Conversations on Faith

On March 3, 2016, I rang the doorbell at the Scorsese residence for the first conversation in what would become a wide-ranging dialogue that took place over the course of several years. On that day, I was welcomed into the kitchen as if I were part of the family and offered a good coffee. "Italian," my host specified. Helen, Martin's wife, greeted me in the living room and we talked at length before Martin's arrival, sitting on the same couch.

Martin entered the room with a welcoming smile. We immediately began talking about our shared roots. In some ways, we're fellow countrymen. He already knew I'm from Messina, in Sicily. He told me he's from Polizzi Generosa, halfway between Messina and Palermo. Or rather, his grandfather was. But for him, it was clear that his roots are there.

As we talked, we remembered his life as the grandson of immigrants in the neighborhoods of New York, his life as an altar boy. Always, there were blood ties, violence, and sacredness. For Martin, church rituals were dramatic, and liturgies were beautiful. Church memories blended with those of a boy who, unknowingly, turned the streets into his first film set: the one of his imagination, dreams, and nightmares, where characters included gangsters and priests.

Two years later, in 2018, I witnessed Martin when he came to Rome to present a book to which he had contributed to Pope Francis.

On that occasion, he publicly asked Francis a question. "Holy Father, today people struggle to change, to believe in the future. They no longer believe in good. We look around, read the newspapers, and it seems that the life of the world is marked by evil, even by terror and humiliation. How can a human being today live a good and just life in a society where greed and vanity drive action, where power is expressed through violence? How can I live well when I experience evil?"

Later, in the Netflix documentary *Stories of a Generation with Pope Francis* (2021), Martin says to his daughter, "We who make movies don't do it for ourselves, but to do justice to the life around us and answer the question of what it means to be human."

When we talked about compiling this book of conversations about faith, I had the impression that for Martin, this is a single, long dialogue in stages. There is a deep thread that unites our words. It's a thread that accompanies me through the maze of life and explores a lifelong preoccupation of Martin's that is present in all of his work.

Antonio Spadaro

Conversations on Faith

Conversation One

Let's start with your childhood. It is well documented that you have suffered from asthma. I find it interesting that Pope Francis also had a problem with his lungs. It seems to me, when you are short of breath you become more sensitive. What was that like growing up? Have you learned something from this shortness of breath?

The first thing to say about asthma is that when it's severe, you really feel like you can't catch your breath. Quite literally, you feel like you could pass away, like you're actually making a passage. There were times when there was just no way to breathe, and the wheezing was so strong, and my lungs were so congested that I started wondering: if this is the way it's going to be from now on, how can I continue? That does go through your mind: you just want some peace.

I developed serious asthma at the age of three. When I was young, back in the fifties, there was a certain way of dealing with doctors, at least for people like my parents. You believed whatever the doctor said – you never went to get a second opinion. Even if they'd wanted to seek out a second opinion, they probably couldn't have afforded one. And the doctors had a certain way of dealing with asthma: there were drugs and treatments, but more importantly there was the imposition of a certain lifestyle. You could not play any sports. You could not exert yourself. They even warned about excessive laughter. And I was allergic to everything around me – animals, trees, grass – so I couldn't go to the country.

All of this meant that I lived a life apart – I felt separate from everyone else. I spent a lot more time with the adults, and it gave me an awareness and, I think, a heightened understanding of the adult world. I had an awareness of the rhythm of life, the concerns of the adults, the discussions of what's right and what's wrong, of one person's obligation to another, and so on. It made me more aware of how people were feeling, more aware of their body language – again, the difference between words and actions – more aware of their sensitivity, which, in turn, helped me cultivate my own sensitivity. I became sharpened, I think.

The memories of looking at the world from my window, looking down on the street and seeing so much – some of it beautiful and some of it horrifying and some of it beyond description – are central for me.

The other side of it is an intensity of focus when I'm at work, staying fixed on what's important. I think that my separateness, my solitude, and my awareness led to a determination and an ability to shut out everything extraneous, which is what happens when I make a film. It's paradoxical, because it's a concentration that protects a sensitivity which results in a kind of insensitivity.

But you weren't always set on filmmaking. After all, you spent some time in a seminary preparatory school. Did you feel a calling, a vocation, to the priesthood? And is being a priest related to being a filmmaker?

Let me start to answer that question by talking about the first big change in my life, which came when I was very young. We were living for a time in Queens, which had trees, space, light – I remember it as a kind of paradise. For my parents, it was like moving to the country. But, because of some family problems, we were evicted back to the Lower East Side of Manhattan, to the Italian-American-Sicilian neighborhood known as Little Italy. We lived there from the forties through the sixties. And, as anyone who has seen a few of my pictures knows, it had a profound effect on me. The contrast between the two places was a traumatic shock.

On each side of the family, my father's side and my mother's side, there were seven or eight children. So, I had many aunts and uncles. They were all born on Elizabeth Street in the early 1900s. Not in a hospital, but right there in the tenements.

They had basically re-created the old country here in the new world. In a very real sense, I grew up in the old world. It was very much like the little villages outside Palermo. My mother's family came from Ciminà, my father's from Polizzi Generosa. Where we lived, everybody was either Sicilian or Neapolitan – with the odd few Calabrese.

My father had four brothers, and my uncle Joe was the youngest. He lived below us on Elizabeth Street with his wife and kids. My grandparents – my father's parents – lived two doors down, and every night my father would go there to see them. They would discuss family matters, the honor of the Scorsese name, the kind of thing I just didn't understand – these were old world matters, and I was born here, in New York.

These were decent people, trying to live a decent life. Everything was built around the family. The family structure was the unifying factor, a way of maintaining decency. Now, organized crime was also present in this world, so people had to walk a tightrope – you couldn't be with them, but you couldn't be against them either. My uncle tended to be with them. He was smalltime, just like Johnny Boy in *Mean Streets* (1973) – forever in trouble. He went to jail a number of times and always owed money to loan sharks. There was a sense of violence present at all times. It was a rough area – a very, very difficult place. It was "street," as we used to say it – "street-tough." A way of being. Everything was built around the family. The family structure was the unifying factor, a way of maintaining decency. This was true for my mother and father, my aunts and uncles.

So, my father took it upon himself to help my uncle. Every day, in that apartment in Little Italy, I could see my father experiencing this: how to deal with his brother in a way that was right and just. He took it all on himself. My mother would get very frustrated at times, and she would say, "Can't your brothers help?" But they had all moved out of the neighborhood. My father and Joe were the only ones left. So, my father dealt with it all himself, and that meant dealing with everyone, on all sides: reasoning, negotiating, making deals, making sure he didn't get taken out, sometimes giving Joe money. He really put himself on the line for my uncle. And it was always about obligation: the obligation to take care of his brother. It was all on us. I loved Joe, but it was very, very tough. It really raised the question: am I my brother's keeper? This question is what I was dealing with in *Mean Streets*.

The place where we were living was, one could say, indecent and profane. There was organized crime, and it affected absolutely everyone. In addition to organized crime, there were also the homeless men and women on the Bowery, people who were really at the end of life, many of them alcoholic, the down and completely out – we got to know some of them, but they always frightened us. Sometimes kids would taunt them, and I saw how easy it was to slip into dehumanizing others, especially when they frighten you. We were frightened by everything, basically. For me, that world was very, very difficult. As I look back on it, I realize my asthma almost brought me a kind of a relief. The pressure to prove yourself with faux masculinity was intense, but my asthma meant I had to find a way to use my head in order to stay alive.

Around the corner from us was the first Catholic cathedral in New York, Old Saint Patrick's, which is now the basilica. It was dedicated in 1815. I was thrown into the Catholic school there by my parents. "Go around the corner, go to school," they said. I spent a lot of time in that church. My family wasn't very religious, but I just found comfort there because the streets were so rough.

At that time, the pastor and many of the priests were from the old generation. It was mainly Italian. In fact, they hardly spoke English. So, we felt quite distant from them. Then around 1953, a young priest came in. His name was Francis Principe and it was his first parish. He was twenty-three years old, and he brought us a whole new way of looking at life. He would get annoyed with me because I wouldn't play any sports – at first, he didn't quite understand that I was told I couldn't play any sports; that if I did, I'd get sick and wouldn't be able to breathe. But apart from that, he represented a way of thinking and a way of dealing with life that was very, very different from the kind of harsh, judgmental, cruel world around me.

He would look at us and say, "You don't have to live like this." He gave us books by Graham Greene. We started with *The Power and the Glory*. The best for me was *The Heart of the Matter*, which was more spiritually and morally complex. Father Principe gave us the essays of Dwight Macdonald, which at that time, in the early fifties, was rather ... unusual, to put it mildly. I somehow found my way to James Joyce, to *Dubliners* and then to *A Portrait of the Artist as a Young Man*, which both had a lasting effect on me. And at that time, the civil rights movement was becoming more prominent and gathering momentum, and I sort of stumbled onto James Baldwin, whose voice really made a difference. I grew up in this enclosed world and I had rarely crossed paths with

African Americans, aside from a few people down on the Bowery.

Father Principe gave us an opening to the world. He played music for us. He loved cinema and recommended movies. And he made sense. He made sense morally. We were being taught these street lessons that came from the old world, and he counterbalanced all of that. He gave us a new way of thinking. His effect on me was powerful, and it made me realize that I couldn't really continue to exist the way I had, in the circumstances around me. There weren't many opportunities open to us. You could be a tough guy; you could be in organized crime – that was wide open to everyone. But that wasn't for me. For a few of my friends, yes. But it wasn't for me.

Now is where I get back to your original question. When I was an adolescent, I found everything in my world so difficult to deal with. Father Principe gave me a kind of clarity, and he also gave me an example of love that was entirely different from the love of my parents. It was a very strong example of love. I wanted to be like him, so I decided that I wanted to be a priest. For my first year of high school, I went to Cathedral College, which was a preparatory seminary. Within two months I knew that it wasn't for me. I stopped studying and behaved like a class clown.

I started to realize that loving someone and wanting to be like them isn't enough – you have to have a vocation. A true vocation is a serious thing. It's not, "I wanna be like that person." He would always tell us, "In order to have a vocation you must love the Mass." I didn't know what he meant. I was an altar boy, and I was always late, and he'd get mad at me. I really didn't understand. In the end, I was invited to leave.

I realized that I was trying to hide by becoming a priest. I was trying to hide from life, and from fear – fear of being hurt, fear of hurting others. And maybe I thought I could create the vocation, control the situation myself. But that's not the way it happens. It's quite the opposite: it's about giving up control and opening yourself up to what can become true love, constant and understanding – the mystery of God's love. You have to explore that and understand that and accept that you may not ever get there. Because the opening and the exploring is what it's all about – the mystery will always remain a mystery, and it's not something to be solved but to be confronted and contemplated.

I recently came across a critic writing about your "obsession with the spiritual." Do you agree that you are "obsessed" with the spiritual dimension of life?

There's something Marilynne Robinson wrote in her book, *Absence of Mind*, that gets right to the heart of this question for me: "The givens of our nature – that we are brilliantly creative and as brilliantly destructive, for example – persist as facts to be dealt with even if the word 'primate' were taken to describe us exhaustively." Of course she's right. The idea that everything can be scientifically explained doesn't seem ridiculous to me, but quite naïve. My own particular struggle has been trying to work through my absorption in my work, my self-absorption, in order to be present for the people I love.

Living in the world of notoriety and fame and ambition and competition is another struggle for me. I've told this story before, but when the Academy Awards were first televised, there was a huge Oscar statuette on stage. It was enormous. And we all watched the show at home and came in to school the next day, excited, but Father Principe saw it differently. He asked, "Did you see that image on television?" And we were confused. But he told us it was the Golden Idol. The statuette was Moloch. He showed us that success was being worshipped.

But, of course, when you're part of that world – I have to admit that I am, to a certain extent, and I've even made a few films about it – the spiritual dimension of life, as you call it, is always right there. Carl Jung had a Latin inscription carved over the doorway to his house in Switzerland: *Vocatus atque non vocatus deus aderit*. Called or not called, God will come. That says it all. I express all of this – everything we're discussing – in cinema.

Conversation Two

I read that at one time, you thought of going to Rome to shoot documentaries on the lives of the saints. Why did this idea come to mind?

In 1981, I had just made *Raging Bull*, and I literally thought it would be my last film. At the time, because of the films that Bertolucci and the Tavianis and others had made for RAI (Radiotelevisione Italiana) and, in particular, Roberto Rossellini's historical films, I thought that television was the future of cinema. Or, I should say: television mixed with cinema was the future. Something entertaining, but with more depth that could teach in some way. Again, this comes from the inspiration of Rossellini. He actually referred to those pictures as "didactic films."

So, I thought RAI was going to be a place where I could explore a question that has always obsessed me: what is a saint?

My idea was to make a series of films about different saints, including saints that might not even have existed, who might have been figures of folklore, taking us back to pre-Judeo-Christian times. I wanted to know where did those figures come from? Why the need for that kind of intercession? For example, St. Christopher, the patron saint of traveling, who, it turns out, did not exist. I suppose when one travels, one is in danger, so there's a need for something or someone to protect us.

But more than that, what about the real saints? How do they relate to people, in general and spiritually? What was their day-to-day life like? What did it consist of? My interest in this goes back to a book that Father Principe gave us, about a modern-day Saint Francis, called *Mr. Blue* by Myles Connolly. Through his protagonist, J. Blue, Connolly tries to show that you can live a good life, not in the material sense, but in terms of decency in the modern world. It reminded me of

Dorothy Day and what she did at the *Catholic Worker*, rejecting materialism, being of service to the poor, and commenting on some of the main issues of the twentieth century. A side note about Dorothy Day, Father Principe once invited her down to a communion breakfast to talk for a small group of elders. I just got a glimpse of her as she was leaving.

Another film that dealt with this question of being a saint in the modern world was *Europa '51* (1952), also by Rossellini, which I saw in a cut version, and was quite influential on me. At the end of the film, the character of Irene – a wealthy Roman housewife who faces a spiritual reckoning after experiencing tremendous tragedy – finds a great peace with herself, and she finds herself of great use. I didn't know at the time that Rosellini was inspired by the French philosopher and mystic Simone Weil, who emphasized self-sacrifice and deep engagement with the lives of the working class. (Simone, however, was not merciful with herself and died in part from voluntary starvation.) I've always been fascinated by figures like this, including saints like Francis, Catherine, and Therese. How they weren't quite activists, but they lived a life in imitation of Christ in the modern world. So that picture was enormously important for me. So was his *The Flowers of St. Francis* (1950), which is the most beautiful film I've ever seen about being a saint.

So, these things were developing for me as I made *Raging Bull*, which, as I said, I meant to be a sign-off from big-budget studio moviemaking.

As it happened, things went differently, and I didn't make the short films for RAI. Instead, I went back to New York and made another picture with Robert De Niro, *The King of Comedy* (1982). Then, I tried to make *The Last Temptation of Christ* (1988), based on the novel by Nikos Kazantzakis, and it fell apart. The reason I changed course was that industry had changed, and it didn't seem possible to make these pictures, these studies, of the lives of the saints. But I never lost my interest in these characters who tried to live their lives in imitation of Christ, and I knew I would return to them one day. In the meantime, a lot of that energy and those discussions went into *Last Temptation* when we finally got to make it a few years later. And, of course, it continued and developed over the years that I lived with *Silence* (2016).

It is not an easy time to have faith in God, in God's love. Pope Francis preaches God with his mercy whose name is mercy. Do you have hope that people today can still feel his presence, and what is mercy to you?

At the beginning of *Mean Streets*, Harvey Keitel says, "You don't make up for your sins in church." Meaning, if you don't lead a truly Christian life, then church is not where you make up for your sins. You do it in the streets and you do it at home and if you say that you do it once a week in church and in confession then you're lying to yourself.

Transubstantiation can't happen only in a building. It has to resonate throughout the rest of the world. And in order for that to happen, we ourselves have to take responsibility for making it happen, through our own actions. In other words, we have to take Jesus and God out of the church and into the streets and into our homes most of all. For me, this is a necessity – it's reality. Have I succeeded, in my own life? I don't know. I don't think so. I'm in my eighties now and I just don't know. But then, maybe "success" is the wrong way of framing it. You just try, and when you fail, you keep trying.

When I was a teenager, I started to become aware of the fact that every Saturday night, we were all going out, drinking, carousing all night long, then showing up for 12:30 Mass on Sunday. As if we could do whatever we wanted and then it would all be okay because we were going to church the next day. There were so many desperate people around the neighborhood. There was a man who was known as a great thief, and he used to walk in the procession of San Rocco. He was praying for the strength to steal more. When you tell the story, it sounds funny. But at the heart of it is a man who was so desperate that he was praying to God to let him do wrong. He felt like he had no choice. How can we judge him?

So, for me, transubstantiation has to happen outside the church. Going to church has to become more than paying weekly installments on an ethical insurance policy. And it's so important for the laity to take part in this effort, to find their way of incorporating God into their hearts.

You know, I'm struck by the fact that we constantly see and hear the words "justice and mercy, justice and mercy" everywhere. And I wonder: shouldn't mercy be first? Because justice can easily, so easily, become a cry for blood, for retribution, and more and more and on and on until the world ends. At some point, it has to stop.

Is compassion instinct or love?

I think the key is the denial of the self. The trap that Charlie falls into in *Mean Streets* is the trap of thinking that his care for Johnny Boy can be his penance, for his own redemption, his own spiritual use. Again, this gets back to the question of the good priests I knew who always put their egos aside. Once you do that, there's only need – the needs of others – and questions of choosing penance or what compassion is or isn't fall away.

They become meaningless.

Conversation Three

We human beings are many things: there is good and bad, there is also violence. There is a lot of violence in your films. You seem to want to stage real, not artificial, grotesque violence. So why? What does violence teach us?

Well, as you mentioned in one of your earlier questions, I am obsessed by the spiritual. I'm obsessed by the question of what we are. And that means looking at us closely, the good and the bad. Can we nurture the good so that at some future point in the evolution of mankind, violence will, possibly, cease to exist? Maybe. But right now, violence is here. It's something that we do. It's important to show that, so that one doesn't make the mistake of thinking that violence is something that others do – that "violent people" do. "I could never do that, of course." Well, actually, you could. We can't deny our nature.

Violence is, for me, a part of being human. The humor in my pictures is from the people and their reasoning, or their lack thereof. Violence, and the profanity of life. Earthiness, if you want to be polite about it. Profanity and obscenity exist, which means that they're part of human nature. It doesn't mean that therefore we are inherently obscene and profane – it means that this is one possible way of being human. It's not a good possibility, but it's a possibility.

Some people just don't understand violence, because they come from cultures, or actually subcultures, from which it's very distant. But I grew up in a place where it was a part of life, and where it was very close to me. Today, many people are growing up in very violent places. I'm not even talking about the parts of the world that are at war, which is a horror. I'm talking about all the random mass shootings in the US, which have happened so often that we take them for granted. Never did I think that we would be facing such a reality, but we are. So, it's an extremely violent life for a lot of people.

In my case, the physical violence I saw around me and that I experienced was overshadowed by the emotional violence: in a way, that was even more terrifying. I think that there are two aspects to violence and its presence in my films. The major, major point is who we are. Violence comes from within us, it's part of the human condition. To deny that only prolongs the situation and puts off any way of reckoning with it. We have to face it in order to understand that it's within our human nature. There are many people I've encountered who are very sweet, and I wonder: what happens when they discover violence within themselves? Unless they're prepared for it, it will come as a shock. To understand that, and to possibly overcome its effects – this is the key.

Back in the early seventies, we were coming out of the Vietnam era and the end of the decorum of old Hollywood. With *Bonnie and Clyde* (1967) and then, really, with *The Wild Bunch* (1969), everything opened up. Those were the pictures that spoke to us, not necessarily in a pleasant way.

About twenty years ago, I was in Washington with the Dalai Lama. I was speaking to a Tibetan monk who was travelling with him, and he said, "I saw your film *Gangs of New York*." I said, "Oh, I'm afraid that it's a little violent . . ." And he said, "Oh, don't be upset about it – it's your nature." I was suddenly very moved. Yes, it might be my nature. That's fine. But then I have to deal with it. We have to know that we're capable of it. That's where we begin to understand it.

There was a writer who recently came to see my film *Killers of the Flower Moon* (2023). The film is based on a great nonfiction book by David Grann that reads like a novel. Around the turn of the twentieth century, the Osage struck oil on their reservation. Pretty quickly, they became some of the richest people in the world.

Then, of course, the white speculators, and swindlers, and opportunists, and thieves, and outright murderers descended – some were "officially sanctioned," you might say, most weren't. They just smelled easy money. So, there was a concentrated effort to kill off pretty much all of the Osage community for their oil money, by every means imaginable: shootings, bombings, hard liquor, and slow poisoning – white men were marrying Osage women and then "helping" the women to die so they could inherit their property and their oil rights. It came to be known as the Osage Reign of Terror, and with good reason.

At any rate, I was talking to this writer, a famous man, and I said, "This man married this woman, they were in love with each other, they had children together . . . and then he started poisoning her. Does that mean that we're all capable of doing such a thing? It's unimaginable." And he said, "Well, if one person is capable of doing it, then we're all capable of doing it." I found that frightening. But true.

The point is, if you understand the violence, you can go one way and make it into a kind of heightened aesthetic experience, the way that Sam Peckinpah did in *The Wild Bunch*. The violence in that picture comes as a shock to the system, and part of the shock is the allure of it, the terrible beauty, the orgasmic release, so to speak. It's extremely stylized, but somehow it reflects the impact and the exhilaration of real violence – the kind of exhilaration that the soldiers involved in the My Lai massacre probably felt. *The Wild Bunch* came out of the Vietnam era, and it really spoke to all the confusion, outrage, and horror we were feeling as a country.

But for me, I don't know any other way to shoot violence except as I saw it. The ugliness of violence, the awkwardness, which Rainer Werner Fassbinder did so well in his early films – that was what I saw in my neighborhood. But growing up there, I also had my own attraction to violence. That gets back to what the monk said to me about *Gangs of New York* (2002). If you grow up around it, it's not so surprising that you might develop some kind of attraction to it. Again, this is something that we have to understand and face in ourselves. We have to know and deal with that truth about ourselves.

In the old neighborhood there were always fights and they could be very exciting, but then there were killings. I didn't witness any murders myself, but I knew some of the people who were killed, and that wasn't funny, it wasn't exciting, and it wasn't beautiful – I can tell you that. I can appreciate the beautiful choreography of violence in the early John Woo pictures, in Zhang Yimou's martial arts films, in *The Grandmaster* (2013) by Wong Kar-wai. But that's ballet. It's phenomenal, but it's ritualized and extremely stylized and it distances you from the reality of violence. I'm not saying that they're wrong, but I am saying that it removes you from the impact of actual violence. John Ford understood violence. So did Sam Fuller. He was an immensely powerful filmmaker.

Every frame of Fuller's movies was teeming with emotional violence, and you felt like it was going to explode any second. I could relate to those pictures.

So, I find that when we distance ourselves from the experience of violence, we do ourselves a real disservice. It seals us off and, most dangerous of all, it creates the illusion that we can eradicate it, keep it at bay, and maybe even inoculate ourselves against it.

What we finally have to do is understand and embrace the violence in ourselves.

Speaking of Killers of the Flower Moon, *this is a film with extreme spiritual tension. Robert De Niro's character, William "Bill" Hale, is a corrupt man mired in a vision of reality marked by evil at its roots. He is a man who lives for lust and dresses up evil with good. On the other hand, Ernest Burkhart, played by Leonardo DiCaprio, is an outspoken young man who only lusts for life, and is always without strategy. Bill insinuates himself into his thoughts and feelings, contaminating his desire for good with the desire for possessions. What is the final difference between each of their methods of doing evil? What is the difference between a corrupt man and a sinner?*

I suppose that what you're talking about is their intentions. What is the difference? And on what level? Spiritual? Moral? One of them has a plan, the other one doesn't, and yet they both do evil. I suppose Dante would have placed Bill lower in the circles of hell than Ernest, but can one really measure degrees of evil? With Ernest, it's a matter of delusion, weakness, avoidance. Yet in the end, Ernest *tries* to redeem himself. He fails, but he tries. Bill, on the other hand, hides behind twisted piousness and righteousness, to the end of his days. So, I think *that's* the difference between them.

DiCaprio's character is one of great complexity and compelling spiritual realism. In your films, you always put the human being before his choices, which are never predictable or obvious. Does the freedom to do good or evil have any real relevance in your films? Or rather, do you believe in a character's "predestination"?

I think it's always important to "put the human being before his choices," as you say. Obviously, as fiction filmmakers, we know what our characters are going to do and how they're going to end up. But in the way we tell the stories, especially in the work with the actors, I find that it's important to keep the mystery of humanity present at all times. Why does someone do what they're doing? Why do they do *this* rather than *that*? This is the mystery. Even to ourselves.

As an aside, I think that filmmakers have gone much deeper into this question since the late forties. That's when the balance of creative power between the director and the actor evened out, and then shifted even further toward the actor. This really began with Elia Kazan's films, with the Actors' Studio and Stella Adler and Sanford Meisner. Things changed. Directors and actors became explorers, working together to illuminate the mystery of being human.

I think that human freedom definitely has relevance in my pictures – otherwise, we wouldn't be talking about redemption. When Father Principe told us, "You don't have to live like this," he was saying: there's another way, another spiritual path that won't just lead out of the neighborhood but that will open your hearts and minds in new and surprising ways. He let us know that we had the freedom to *choose*.

Predestination is something we can only contemplate as an idea. If it exists, it's in a realm and in a form that we will never comprehend. It seems like something that was invented for us to torture ourselves, or to give us a kind of quasi-spiritual alibi: if I'm already damned then I'll just do whatever I want whenever I want. I knew people who assumed this attitude, essentially linking sins they committed against the Holy Spirit with a child's idea of predestination. In other words, they committed a sin that was deemed unforgivable by the church, so they must have been predestined to die unredeemed. But that runs counter to the heart of Jesus' teachings –

the door to redemption is always open. So, no matter how one defines it, I'm not sure that predestination is relevant to the example of Jesus.

Where's the heart of this movie? Where's the emotion? How did the movie change your life? Was there anything that caught you off guard?

When we were preparing the picture, there was a dinner in Gray Horse. I walked in to find 250 members of the Osage community, some in formal ceremonial dress. A big traditional meal. Then people from the community got up to speak. A range of emotions – worry, trepidation, support, sadness, enthusiasm. Slowly, the catastrophe had a face. All these people. They were living it. Their families had experienced it: the murders, the betrayals.

Some people were worried about the violence of some of my pictures, whether or not I was the right person to tell this story. A woman named Brandy Lemon said that she shared their concerns, but that she was reassured when she watched *Silence*. And then, something unexpected happened. Margie Burkhart, the granddaughter of Mollie and Ernest, spoke. She said that the most important thing to remember was that Ernest and Mollie just *loved* each other, that it was a love relationship. It was not as simple as villains and victims.

When she said that, it all changed for me. It was like the scales fell from my eyes. I began to see everything differently. I began to realize that their relationship might very well have been the heart of the story. That it was a microcosm of the whole tragic situation of the reign of terror, a terrible spiral of love and death. To a certain extent, this was also true of Bill's character. Bill spoke Osage, he knew the culture inside and out, his love for them was real. But it was a twisted love, of a terrible father who trades the lives of his children for money and power.

The growing levels of trust and friendship with so many members of the Osage community had a profound effect on me. We never would have made the picture without that kind of bond. And as I got to be with them over so many months, I got to know them as individuals, as people. As real friends. With those friends, an understanding developed, a sense of real trust. Trust. The word is used too often now, and it can lose its meaning and its impact, but that's what it was. We came to trust each other. It was a great gift.

In the film, when the credits roll at the end, you can hear a fly buzzing. Hearing that buzzing sound and watching the black screen made me feel that in the end, Ernest is me, the spectator, called to account for himself.

The flies were there. On set. In one scene, where Ernest gives Mollie the medicine, he senses her drifting away. Dying? He becomes frightened. Then a fly landed on the back of Leo's neck and his immediate reaction was to slap it hard . . . he incorporated the action into the scene, as if Ernest was trying to slap away the evil around him. And we worked with it and repeated it in the first interrogation scene with Tom White, the Bureau of Investigation officer.

Ernest ends up poisoning his love. Do we poison, sometimes, those whom we love? How is this possible?

I think it goes even deeper between Ernest and Mollie as characters. He loved her. She loved him. He knew, on some level, what he was giving her. Yet, she trusted him. Maybe she knew, on a deeper, bodily level, and she kept it from herself. Sometimes it goes that far between people. More than we know, I think. How is it possible? I suppose that many people create a narrative for themselves that screens out things they don't want to see and emotions they don't want to feel, but that are happening anyway. Truths that are too unbearable, that contradict the way everything was *supposed* to go. It's hard to accept.

But it's true.

Why do you appear at the end of the film? Who is Scorsese in this film?

The radio, as a device, relocated us, took us into a realm of pure simplistic entertainment. It had to be something that removed us from the story *we* were telling and shifted to the story of the murders as it came to be told and then lost in the culture. Or maybe I should say *by* the culture. The sensationalized version, keeping the thrills and the intrigue and leaving out all the pain, the sorrow, the genuine tragedy of the Osage reign of terror. This is based on the actual radio shows of the period. All that tragedy reduced for easy consumption to a 22-minute radio show touting the FBI.

It did become a radio show in the thirties, and now it's a movie in 2023, and I was the filmmaker. We shot the scene in my old high school, Cardinal Hayes; I didn't cast the role of the radio show producer because deep down I sensed it had to be me. I was uncertain, but I decided to try. My family was there watching. I spoke of

Mollie being laid to rest beside her father, her mother, her sisters, and her daughter, with my wife, my daughter, and my granddaughter nearby – and as I repeated the words, take after take, the rhythm and the resonance of the words started to set in and take effect, and it seemed to feel very natural and sad.

After all, I came to this story as a part of the greater society outside the Osage, the society that had dominated and almost destroyed this people and their culture. That conferred a kind of culpability on me, and I accepted the responsibility of addressing it head on. So, I felt that it was right to go before the camera and speak directly to the audience. When I come in, the façade drops, the tone changes, everything slows down, and it's me speaking to the audience. I'm saying, these were real people, this really happened, and . . . then, the final line: there was no mention of the murders.

And that opened the way for the final shot of the drum circle, which is completely contemporary. It's like blood pumping through a body, the

Osage culture as a living organism, despite everything, despite all those deaths, all that horror.

This isn't a gangster story. The criminals here aren't part of any tight-knit, exclusive clique that requires special initiation. This was a public conspiracy, reminding us that the bad guys don't always lose. We are in 2023. Wars and violence inflame the world. The world order is in crisis. Back in 2014, when speaking at a memorial for Italian soldiers, Pope Francis lamented, "Even today, after the second failure of another world war, perhaps one can speak of a third war, one fought piecemeal, with crimes, massacres, destruction." What does Killers of the Flower Moon *say in the context of what Pope Francis calls the "third world war in pieces"?*

Killers is ultimately about power. Power fueled by greed. Power is the ultimate temptation. It's always being fought for somewhere. Look at the last forty years. The Soviets in Afghanistan. The horrendous war between Iran and Iraq. Our invasion of

Iraq, where almost everything went wrong. The nightmare in Syria. Ukraine. And on and on. It's constant.

It comes back to this question of the violence in ourselves. We tend to look away from it. We deny it. We tell ourselves that we're above it. We comfort ourselves with the fantasy that it has nothing to do with us. I feel that the only real hope is change from within, one human being at a time. And we have to start by confronting the possibility of violence within us.

The Osage reign of terror was a matter of power and greed. It was very easy for Bill Hale and all the other murderers to dehumanize the Osage, but these men and women weren't murdered because they were Osage, they were murdered for their money. In the end, the murderers didn't get away with anything *but* money. The Osage have their extraordinary culture, now in the process of being reborn and reconstructed.

Before we go, I have one last thought about love and the depth of understanding of people who are extremely violent. There was a very interesting review of *The Irishman* (2019) in a British literary supplement that I enjoy reading. It was by a very good writer. He wrote that he liked certain aspects of the film, but he found it odd that I was concerned with Frank's soul since I hadn't provided any "clues about his inner life." Not to be defensive, but I think he missed the point.

We learn about the inner lives of others by observing their outer behavior and by talking to them. With a guy like Frank, with all of those people in that world, they don't talk about anything. Frank's inner life is expressed in his eyes, in his pauses and silences, his hesitations, in the way he holds things back. But talking? Self-examination? That urge only starts to open up within him near the end, almost unconsciously – the weight becomes too much for him to bear.

So, I felt that a moral judgment was being made by this writer, and within that judgment was an implication that some souls are less worthy of concern than others. But gangsters are human beings, so it's not a matter of gangsters per se, it's all of us. It's who we are. Of course it's troubling, and it's inconvenient. People think, "How can I possibly be put in the same category as a murderer? They're just gangsters, they're just drug addicts, they're just lowlifes." No. You can't just dismiss a whole great swath of humanity like that. They are us.

Conversation Four

For you, believing in God and being a Catholic are two distinct things. Have I understood that correctly? Can you explain what you mean by that?

Well, I'm interested in how people perceive God, or, I should say, how they perceive the world of the intangible. There are many pathways, and I think that the one you choose depends on what culture you're a part of. My way has been, and is, Catholicism. After many years of thinking about other things, dabbling here and there, I am most comfortable as a Catholic. I believe in the tenets of Catholicism. I'm not a doctor of the church. I'm not a theologian who could argue the Trinity. I'm certainly not interested in the politics of the institution. But the idea of the Resurrection, the idea of the Incarnation, the powerful message of compassion and love – that's the key. The sacraments, if you are allowed to take them, to experience them, help you stay close to God.

Now, I realize that this begs the question: am I a practicing Catholic? If that means "Are you a regular churchgoer?" then the answer is no. But then, as I've said, at an early age I came to believe that practicing is not something that happens only in a consecrated building during certain rituals performed at a certain time of day. Practicing is something that happens outside, all the time. Practicing, really, is everything you do, good or bad, and reflecting on it. That's the struggle. However, the comfort and the profound impression of Catholicism at a very early age . . . I'll say that it's something that I've always related back to.

This calls to mind a beautiful gift you once gave me, the book The Practice of the Presence of God *by Brother Lawrence, a Carmelite friar who lived in the seventeenth century. What struck me was the reference to the fact that he "receives divine assistance at all times and places." He is used to the constant presence of God: "To be with God, it is not necessary to be always in church. We may make a chapel of our heart." Also: "He is no longer troubled by the necessity of seeking and finding [the presence of God]; it is always there, for him to take whenever he pleases." And finally: "It was a great delusion to imagine that prayer time should be different from any other." How did you learn about this book? What struck you about it?*

I had seen a talk on YouTube given by the English spiritual teacher Rupert Spira. Someone asked him a question about eternity, and he made the point that it isn't off in the distance, like a place we journey to after we die. Spira said that the past is always behind us and the future is always ahead of us and unknowable – we created the ideas of the past and the future to give ourselves a sense of structure. Yet all that really exists is right here and right now, which we can never grasp. So, in essence, we dwell in eternity. This stayed with me.

I told my friend, the filmmaker and writer Kent Jones, about the discussion. He listened to another one of Spira's podcasts where the topic was Christian mystics. Spira talked a lot about Brother Lawrence of the Resurrection, and Kent was intrigued, so he found a copy of his book. He read it through a couple of times and then he found a copy for me, which I read and gave to you.

I was struck by the beautiful simplicity of Brother Lawrence's thought. He wasn't a theorist or a theologian, like Meister Eckhart. He didn't write sermons or tracts. He shared his reflections and experiences in conversations with and in letters to people who came to him for guidance. He wasn't a saint. He was an ex-soldier who'd had a conversion experience at a very young age and become a Carmelite friar, and he did kitchen work in his monastery for most of his life and found meaning in it. In a passage from the book, he says, "The time of business does not with me differ from the time of prayer; and in the noise and clutter of my kitchen, while several persons are at the same time calling for different things, I possess GOD in as great tranquility as if I were upon my knees at the Blessed Sacrament." He lived his faith.

When I was very young, I wondered: what is prayer? What is it for? What is it to pray *for* something? And why is it confined within the four walls of a church? In a sense, Brother Lawrence answered these questions in the living of his own life. Of course that's reflected in the passages that you quote. There's another beautiful passage where he says that he had resolved to make the love of God the end of all his actions, and that he was happy when he could pick up a straw from the ground for the love of God, "seeking Him alone, nothing else, not even His gifts." In other words, all of life is prayer, and prayer has no object or goal. It is communion with God and it's constant because it is always everywhere. That's remarkable.

You also advised me to watch two films by the Dardenne brothers, The Son *(2002) and* Rosetta *(1999). I was deeply impressed by these two films. Both endings are exceptional. Why did you recommend them to me? How do you feel about these films?*

I admire the Dardenne brothers. They admit and dramatize the possibility of redemption, which has haunted and obsessed me for most of my life. They don't look away from ugliness or the tough aspects of life around them, but the possibility of redemption is always there for their characters. When it comes, it's always awkwardly, tentatively, the way it is in life. You could say that they make "spiritual suspense films," about people living on the very edge of life who somehow find their way. And they don't seem to be good or bad, they're just people, struggling to do *more* than just survive. They get a glimpse of the light, and they stumble ahead and open the door – to others. That's very moving to me. Their pictures are difficult to watch, yet they're moving and inspiring.

Well, time flies, but I would like to stay with you for hours and hours. I've learned a lot from you, I have to say. Now, my last question for today is:

what is God's grace to you? How do you experience the grace of God?

That's a hard question. You said that you've learned from me, which, coming from you, is a great compliment. Of course, I wasn't teaching, I was just talking. As you know, I don't have a theological background, so when I'm talking it's always from lived experience.

I do know that all the denial and the rejection that I've gotten has been a form of grace for me. To begin again, and again, and again. In 1978, I was literally almost dead in a hospital. Somehow, I made it through, got up, and began again. I remember telling the story of that time in my life to a man named Hyemeyohsts Storm. He looked at me and he said, "In that hospital you died. You're now resurrected." He's a controversial figure in the native community, but . . . he was right. He was right about this.

In November of 1963, two weeks before Kennedy was shot, I got into the back of a car owned by this off-duty cop, a guy we knew. In my neighborhood, nobody had a car except the wise guys. You wanted to go somewhere, you took the subway. Cars weren't part of the culture, so it was kind of a novelty for us. This guy behaved brashly, and he had a gun that he brandished openly. You never showed guns in the neighborhood, and you never wore a gun. It was very dangerous. But he had a police badge, he had this swagger, he had his gun, he had his convertible, and we were so bored that we got in and drove around with him. He was behaving boorishly but we put up with it. We thought, "Oh, this guy has a car and maybe we can go for a coffee somewhere uptown or maybe even upstate for an hour, at least it's something." I was at New York University then, trying to read Henry James. At the same time, I was still living with my parents on Elizabeth Street. It was a split existence.

There was another guy in the front seat, so my friend Joe and I rode in the back. There was a lot of activity on the streets that night, lots of drinking in the after-hours clubs, the illegal clubs. It was one in the morning and in those days, it was dark –

in '63 there were no lights in the doorways around the city, in any of the buildings, that only happened a couple of years later. We were driving around, and suddenly the guy slammed on the brakes. There was a car in front of us, blocking the way. He blew his horn. No response. He blew the horn again. Nothing. Then he got out and went up to the driver in the next car, and they got into a big argument, and then this guy flashed his badge and showed his gun. The other driver just said, "Okay." The guy got back in with us; the other car drove off. Joe looked at me and said, "Forget it, this guy's acting like a fool. We should just call it a night."

So, we said goodnight, we went home, and the guy and his friend drove away. Within five minutes, they were shot up on Astor Place. The kid in the front got his eye shot out. I found out the next morning. I ran into Joe, and he said, "We're living on borrowed time. Nobody knows we were in that car, so don't say anything. Thank God we got out." Why did that happen? We would have been killed, or severely maimed at the very least.

I realized: I don't belong here. But it was hard

for us to just get up and leave and start a new life – that seems difficult for people to understand now, I think, but it was true. You had to utilize what you had, build from it. I had Father Principe's guidance. I was getting an education at NYU. At the time, a revolution in cinema was bursting out all over the world. There was the new lightweight camera and sound equipment that gave all of us the ability to make our own movies. I was open to all of it, and everything pointed in the direction of cinema – a way out, my way, my path. And this experience, where I came so close to being killed, became a guide of some kind, maybe even a demand for me to do something.

So, I poured everything I felt and experienced, all of my questioning, my search for Jesus, my love for the church and my family, the people around me, all of it went into the creation of *Mean Streets*, *Raging Bull*, *Casino* (1995) – really, all of my pictures, in one way or another. And somehow, I was able to make a career out of these films that, for the most part, I really wanted to make. The trade-off is that while you get the recognition, you also have to put up with the periods of rejection – of being "washed-up," as they used to say in Hollywood – and you have to keep coming back. So, I received the grace of being rejected, the grace of being despised, and the gift of saying: "Okay, now we're going to start all over again."

You have claimed to have lived on the edge of destruction, to have almost hit bottom. What is salvation for you?

There's a deception in self-destruction: that in order to understand destruction, you have to destroy yourself. It somehow becomes a kind of arrogance, a pride, and then, you've destroyed yourself. In my case, I came out of a self-destructive moment in my life, somehow – I got there naïvely and came out of it just as naïvely.

When I was an altar boy, I served at funerals and at the Saturday Solemn High Mass for the dead, and I had a friend whose father was an undertaker. I watched the older generation that came over from Sicily at the turn of the century die away, and that was a profound experience for me. I thought a lot about mortality – just not my own. And at a certain point, I did quite a bit of damage to myself. When I came out of it, the first picture I made was *Raging Bull*. I found that I was more understanding and compassionate in my heart toward this very tough character. I was more open to Jake LaMotta and I didn't care about what people would think. It wasn't about identification. It was a matter of openness and acceptance.

So, the other side of this question is about accepting yourself, living with yourself, and possibly becoming a force for something positive in people's lives. I suppose that's one way of defining salvation. It comes down to the people you love: your family, your friends, your loved ones. You try to be as good as you can, and as reasonable and compassionate as you can. But along the way, you also learn something else. In *Ride the High Country* (1962) by Sam Peckinpah, there's a scene where Edgar Buchanan, a drunken minister, is marrying Mariette Hartley's character to this man, and he says, "You've got to understand something about marriage – people change." The same thing goes for every relationship. It goes for collaborations. Over time, people you know very well and who you've worked with for a very long time might have other needs, other things that become important to them, and you have to recognize that. You accept who they are, you accept how they've changed, you try to nurture what's best. And sometimes, you have to recognize that they have to go find their own way. There was a time when I considered that a betrayal. But then I realized that it wasn't: it was just change.

The word "salvation" is interesting. Because it's something that one can never know. At the moment of your death, if you're conscious, do you know if you've reached salvation? How do you know? You certainly can't know while you're living. The only thing you can do is to live as decent a life as you can. If you fall, you have to pick yourself up and try again – a cliché, but it's true. For me, day and night, there are peaks and valleys, constant exhilaration and darkness, a doubting that becomes self-criticism.

But you can't overdo that because, again, you have to accept yourself. So, it's an ongoing process.

Conversation Five

Let's talk about another movie. What did Silence *mean to you? Did it have an impact on your life? Both in thinking about it and in making it? And do you view it as a step forward from* The Last Temptation of Christ?

Both films were incredibly important to me. Getting them made was very difficult and in both cases the budgets and the schedules were tight.

At one point late in the process of making *The Last Temptation of Christ*, we organized a screening of the rough cut for people from different religious groups. The people behind the film were there, of course – my producers, my editor Thelma Schoonmaker, and Tom Pollack, who was running Universal at the time. My old friend Father John

Keenan came along with us. He and I were in the preparatory seminary together.

It was a very tense situation, because the film was already extremely controversial, before anyone had actually seen it. There were people in that room who were going to hate it, and we knew that. Before the film started, I got up and said a few words about the picture, I explained that it wasn't quite finished, and I said that after the film there would be a gathering and whoever wanted to join us for a little dinner and a discussion was welcome. Among all the people who had watched the film, the only two who showed up for the dinner were the Episcopal bishop Paul Moore and his wife. He mentioned that he thought the film was "Christologically correct," which was encouraging.

So, we all sat down and shared a meal and talked. Bishop Moore and I spent quite a bit of time talking to each other about our lives. I told him about growing up where I did. He told me about serving in World War Two, which had a profound effect on his life. I felt that my own experience of life could never even begin to compare to his.

He said, "I'm going to give you a book, it's called *Silence*," and then he described it to me. This was in 1988. I received the book by Shūsaku Endō and I held onto it – I didn't read it right away. I took it with me to Japan in 1989 when I played Van Gogh for Akira Kurosawa in his film *Dreams* (1990). I was late, because I had to finish *GoodFellas* (1990) and we had gone over budget and schedule.

As an aside, I made *GoodFellas* at Warner Brothers because I owed them a film – they had agreed to let me go and make *Last Temptation* at Universal. All the studio heads in Hollywood knew how much I wanted to make that picture and I really drove them crazy! And they made it all work, those guys. It was quite something to see the different studio heads come together and say, "Alright, we'll forgive that debt, go ahead, and when you're done make this other film." Which was *GoodFellas*, and which was also extremely difficult to get off the ground.

At any rate, we were racing to finish and the great master Akira Kurosawa was eighty-two years old and he was waiting for me. I was late! So, I took *Silence* with me, and I read it through for the first time on the bullet train in Japan. The story of Rodrigues – a Portuguese Jesuit priest sent to seventeenth-century Japan, who is forced to choose between following the tenets of his faith and saving the lives of his congregants – was so disturbing, so profound to me, that I didn't know if I could ever even attempt to approach it. But, when I came to the passage where Jesus says, "Step on me," to Rodrigues, I was overwhelmed. If he stepped on the *fumi-e*, a likeness of Jesus on which Christians were forced to step and thereby deny their faith, would he be betraying everything he believed in? In the end, he let Jesus guide him. That was the moment when I realized that I had to make it into a film.

That began a twenty-year odyssey of different producers and different actors, trying to write the script, trying to understand exactly what Endō was going for, the whole concept, and what

Rodrigues, Garrupe, Kichijiro, all of them went through. In addition to that, I had to learn more about Japan's history and the history of the Jesuits in Japan. So, there was a lot to do. During all those years, I started to believe that there was no way I would make the picture. It would have felt . . . presumptuous of me. I didn't know how to deal with the themes.

In retrospect, I think I started writing the script a little too soon. We got stuck on certain scenes and I put it away and went off and made a few other films – quite a few other films. We finally obtained the rights around 1990 and about a year later, my friend and writing collaborator Jay Cocks and I tried to write a draft. But really, I just wasn't ready. It was the beginning of a long process that led to the first real draft of the script in December 2006 – that was when we came up with a real structure for a movie.

The problem then was legal issues. There were so many producers and people that had claims on it, and it took another four or five years before some old friends came aboard and cut through the

Gordian knot of legal claims and issues. This is why you see so many producer credits on that film. They each did something, but in certain cases it was a matter of simply staying with the film for all the years when nothing was happening with it. Then, there was the problem of actors. I'd find actors I liked and who were "bankable" – actors who guaranteed a certain amount of money necessary to make the picture and who actually wanted to play the roles – they agreed to do the picture, and then time would pass, and they were either no longer "bankable" or they were too old, or both. And this whole time I was trying to come to terms with what Rodrigues did, and everything that built to that one moment when he steps on the *fumi-e*.

Then we got to pre-production. We looked at quite a few locations around the world before we settled on Taiwan. We started with the real places in Japan where Shūsaku Endō's novel takes place – Nagasaki, Sotome, Unzen Hot Springs – but we didn't end up filming there because it would have been prohibitively expensive. In addition to Japan, my production designer, Dante Ferretti, scouted

New Zealand, Vancouver, Northern California and then, finally, Taiwan, which has extraordinary landscapes and coastlines that are virtually untouched, and that are visually close to the places in the novel. Right away, we realized that this was where we could make the picture. And Ang Lee suggested Taiwan, too. He said, "Go there, we have everything." We wound up using Hou Hsiao-hsien's sets from *The Assassin* (2015).

The whole experience was extraordinary. The making of *Silence* had an impact on everyone who worked on it. It was another very difficult shoot, even harder than *Last Temptation*. But I never saw people work so hard and with such good humor as they contended with earthquakes, typhoons, and the Taiwanese cobra – apparently, they were in season, which people kept from me. We actually shot in a typhoon, and the Japanese actors who had to get onto the crosses, with the water constantly hitting them, insisted on staying up there. "Come on down," I said. "No, I'll do more shots for you," they said. These were remarkable actors.

And it was a very beautiful experience with

Andrew Garfield and Adam Driver. The night when we shot the scene where Andrew Garfield has to step on the *fumi-e*, the stunt people were playing Christians who were hung upside down in pits . . . and they really were hanging upside down in pits. It was extremely difficult for them. It was around five in the morning when we shot. And the instant he stepped on the *fumi-e*, we heard the cock crow – for real! And Andrew did it so beautifully. It was something that no one who was there will ever forget. It was around six in the morning when we all stumbled back to the hotel. There's still so much in my head about *Silence*, so much about the missionary work at that time that was depicted in the novel. And it connects directly to when I was young, to seeing the behavior and the example of Jesus in the actions of others. In the example that Father Principe set for me, and in the times when I was sick and my mother stayed in the room with me and didn't leave.

"Why is that person that way?" you ask yourself. "Why are they going so far, giving that much of themselves?" Then you start to explore it, and you see the role and the actual presence of faith. And if you have a measure of faith yourself, as I did when I was young, you might go deeper, become more interested. And you might come to understand, one day, that we each have to find our own way to becoming capable of that love. I think that's probably something that Rodrigues finally understood: that his immediate response to the situation he faced, his way of following Jesus, may have been right for his own culture but not for the situation in Japan.

Looking back, I think that the long gestation process for the movie became a way of living with the story, and living life – my own life – around it and around the ideas in the book. I was provoked, by those ideas, to think further about the question of faith. The film has been with me, I've lived with it. So, it's informed everything I've done. Choices I've made. Ways of approaching certain ideas and scenes in other pictures I've made over the years. There was the desire to make the actual film on the one hand, and on the other hand, the presence of the Endō novel, the story, as a kind of spur to thinking about faith, about life and how it's lived, about grace and how it's received, about how they can be the same in the end. All of this, in turn, gave me greater strength and clarity in my approach to the concrete task of making the picture.

I look back and I see it all coming together in my memory as a kind of pilgrimage – that's the way it felt. It's amazing to me, to have received the grace to be able to make the film at that point in my life.

Were there people of faith alongside you who supported you in your research and then in the making of this film?

There were many. Bishop Paul Moore, of course, of the Episcopal Church, St. John the Divine, in New York, who first gave me the novel to read. We screened *Last Temptation* for him, not knowing what his response would be, and he and I had a good dialogue about the picture. Just as he was leaving, he told me he was going to give me a book, which turned out to be *Silence*. Father James Martin, of the Society of Jesus, who worked with Andrew Garfield on his Spiritual Exercises in his preparation for the role, was extremely important to us.

During production, we had the support and encouragement of several priests in Taipei, many of whom served as technical consultants on the film, making sure that Andrew and Adam performed the sacraments authentically. Father Jerry Martinson, SJ (Kuangchi Program Service); Father Alberto Nunez Ortiz, SJ (whom we found through Fu Jen University); and Archbishop Paul Russell and Father Ivan Santus at the Nunciature in Taipei.

We had several historical consultants including two Jesuits who were very helpful in the research for the film: David Collins, SJ, a historian at Georgetown University, and Shinzo Kawamura, SJ, of Sophia University.

Van C. Gessel, a Japanese language professor at Brigham Young University, has translated most of Shūsaku Endō's work into English, and he has been a great supporter of the film and a direct link to Endō. We first consulted with him in 2011.

In 2009, when I visited the Twenty-Six Martyrs Museum in Nagasaki, I met Renzo De Luca, an Argentinian Jesuit who is currently the Provincial of the Japan Province of the Society of Jesus, and he was very helpful in providing the "Madonna of the Snows" scroll that appears in the film. Early on, my researcher met with Antoni Ucerler, SJ.

Our two main historical consultants were both raised Catholic and were involved in the film since 2011. Jurgis Elisonas, an authority on Japan during the Early Modern Era who has written extensively on the historic figure Ferreira, and Liam Brockey, a historian who has written on the topic of seventeenth-century missionaries and their presence in Asia, who is currently President of the American Catholic Historical Association.

Your film, and the choice of a novel like Silence, *seems to go to the roots of Christian spirituality and the Catholic imagination. You could say that it's a film in the style of the French Catholic author Georges Bernanos in a sense. What do you think of that?*

I agree that it goes to the roots of Christian spirituality, but I'm not sure that I agree about the comparison with Bernanos. For me, it comes down to the question of grace. Grace is something that happens throughout life. It comes at unexpected moments. Now, I'm saying that as someone who has never been through war, or torture, or occupation. I've never been tested in that way. Of course, there are those people who were tested, like Jacques Lusseyran, the blind French resistance leader who was sent to Buchenwald and kept the spirit of resistance alive for his fellow prisoners – in fact, we've been trying for many years to make a film based on his memoir, *And There Was Light*. There's Dietrich Bonhoeffer, too. Elie Wiesel and Primo Levi found a way to help others. I'm not saying that their examples provide some kind of definitive answer to the question "Where was God when so many millions of people were systematically slaughtered?" But they existed, they performed acts of tremendous courage and compassion, and we remember them as lights in the darkness.

You can't see through someone else's experience, only your own. So, it might seem paradoxical, but I related to the novel by Endō, in a way that I never have to Bernanos. There's something so hard, so unrelentingly harsh in Bernanos. Whereas in Endō, tenderness and compassion are always there. Always. Even when the characters don't know that tenderness and compassion are there, we do.

You mention God, so I want to ask, who is God for you? Is he the object of punishment and perplexity or the source of joy and harmony? Pope Francis speaks of God as Mercy. He wants to get rid of and repudiate any image of God as a torturer. Can God ever be a torturer?

This brings me back to Bernanos, by way of Robert Bresson and his adaptation of Bernanos's novel, *Diary of a Country Priest* (1951). I saw the film for the first time in the mid-sixties. I was in my early twenties, and I was growing up and moving beyond the idea of Catholicism that I'd held as a child.

Like many people who were raised in the Roman Catholic church at that time, I was overwhelmed and deeply impressed as a child by the severe side of God as he was presented to us – the God that punishes you when you do something bad, the God of storms and lightning. This is what Joyce was dealing with in *A Portrait of the Artist as a Young Man*, too.

It was an extremely dramatic moment in the US, of course. Vietnam was escalating, and it had just been declared a "holy war." So, for me and for many others, there was a lot of confusion and doubt and sadness that was just there, a part of the reality of everyday life. It was at that time that I saw Bresson's *Diary of a Country Priest*, and it gave me hope. Every character in that picture, with the possible exception of the older priest, is suffering. Every character is feeling punished and most of them are inflicting punishment on each other. And at one point, the priest has an exchange with one of his parishioners, and he says to her: "God is not a torturer. He just wants us to be merciful with ourselves."

And that opened something up for me. That was the key. Because even though we feel that God is punishing and torturing us, if we're able to give ourselves the time and space to reflect on it, we realize that we're the ones doing the torturing, and we're the ones we have to be merciful with. I got to meet Bresson once in Paris, and I told him just what the picture meant to me.

After I made *Raging Bull*, I came to realize that this was what we had made – this was what the film was about. We didn't go into that picture with a theme in mind, we just tried to make a film about someone who led a kind of life that we knew, in a world that we knew.

The protagonist, Jake LaMotta, is punishing everyone around him, but the one he's really punishing is himself. So, at the end, when he looks in the mirror, he sees that he has to be merciful with himself. Or, to put it another way, he has to accept himself, and live with himself. And then, maybe it will become easier for him to live with other people, and to receive their goodness.

When I was young, I was extraordinarily lucky, because I had Father Principe. I learned so much from him, and that included mercy with oneself and with others. Of course, he sometimes played the role of the stern moral instructor – his example was something else again. This man was a real guide. He could talk tough, but he never actually forced you to do anything. He guided you. Advised you. Cajoled you. He had such extraordinary love.

Who is the character that intrigues you the most from the novel and in your film? And why?

When I was younger, I was thinking of making a film about being a priest. As you know, I myself wanted to follow in Father Principe's footsteps and be a priest. I realized, at the age of fifteen, that a vocation is something very special, that you can't acquire it, and you can't have one just because you want to be like somebody else. You have to have a true calling. Now, if you do have the calling, how do you deal with your own pride? If you're able to perform a ritual in which transubstantiation is enacted, then yes – you're very special.

However, you have to have something else as well. Based on what I saw and experienced, a good priest, in addition to having that talent, that ability, always has to think of his parishioners first. So, the question is: how does that priest get past his ego? His pride? I wanted to make that film. And I realized that with *Silence*, almost sixty years later, I was making that film. Rodrigues is struggling directly with that question.

But I think that the most fascinating and intriguing of all the characters is Kichijiro, the one who betrays Rodrigues. At times, when we were making the picture, I thought, "Maybe he's Jesus, too." In Matthew, Jesus says: "Just as you did it to one of the least of these who are members of my family, you did it to me." You cross paths with the person in the street who repels you – that's Jesus. Of course, Kichijiro is constantly weakening, and constantly causing damage to himself and to many others, including his family. But then, at the end, who's there with Rodrigues? Kichijiro. He was, it turns out, Rodrigues's great teacher. His mentor. His guru, so to speak. That's why Rodrigues thanks him at the end.

And of course, in terms of my own pictures, people have pointed out to me that Kichijiro is Johnny Boy in *Mean Streets*. The character of Charlie, played by Harvey Keitel, has to get through his pride. He understands that spirituality and practice is not limited to the actual edifice of the literal church, that it has to be outside on the street. But then, of course, you can't choose your own penance. He thinks he can, but penance comes when you least expect it, from a quarter that you can never anticipate. This is why Johnny Boy and Kichijiro fascinate me. They become the vehicle for destruction or salvation.

Are Father Rodrigues and Father Ferreira, who also renounced his faith, two faces of the same coin or are they two different, incomparable coins?

We don't know what the historical Father Ferreira did or didn't believe, but in the Endō novel it would seem that he actually lost his faith. Maybe another way of looking at it is that he couldn't get over the shame of renouncing his faith, even if he did it to save lives. Rodrigues, on the other hand, is someone who renounces his faith and thereby regains it. That's the paradox. To put it simply, Rodrigues hears Jesus speak to him and Ferreira doesn't, and that's the difference.

Silence seems to be the story of a profound discovery of the face of Christ, a Christ who seems to be asking Rodrigues to trample on him for the salvation of others because that is why he came into the world. What is the face of Christ for you? Is it that fumi-e, *the icon trampled on such as Endō described? Or is it the glorious Christ in Majesty?*

I chose the face of Christ painted by El Greco, because I thought it was more compassionate than the one that Endō refers to in the novel, which was painted by Piero della Francesca. When I was growing up, the face of Christ was always a comfort, and a joy.

Was there a situation in which you felt God was close, even if silent?

I was young, and serving Mass, there was no doubt that there was a sense of the sacred. I tried to convey this in *Silence*, during the scene of the Mass in the farmhouse in Goto. At any rate, I remember going out on the street after the Mass was over and wondering: how can life just be going on? Why hasn't everything changed? Why isn't the world directly affected by the body and blood of Christ? That's the way that I experienced the presence of God when I was very young.

In 1983, I was in Israel scouting locations for *Last Temptation*. I was flying around the country in small single engine planes. I don't like to fly at all, particularly in small planes. So, I was holding onto these small religious items that my mother had given me years earlier. I was rigid, very tense. I was going back and forth from Tel Aviv to Galilee to Bethesda to Elat. And at one point I was taken into the church of the Holy Sepulchre. I was there with the producer, Robert Chartoff, who passed away in 2015. When I was at the tomb of Christ, I knelt and said a prayer. I came out, and Bob asked me if I felt anything different. I said that I really didn't, I was just overwhelmed by the geography of the place, and by all the religious orders that had staked a claim there. So, then we had to fly back to Tel Aviv. I got on the plane. Again, I was very rigid, and I was clutching all of these religious items from my mother in my hand. And suddenly, as we were flying, I realized that I didn't feel the need for them anymore.

I just felt an all-encompassing kind of love, and a sense that if anything was going to happen it wasn't going to happen then. It was extraordinary. And I feel lucky enough to have experienced that once in my life.

I also want to talk about the birth of my daughter Francesca. She was delivered by caesarian. I was there, watching everything as it happened. And then, suddenly, I was told to leave. I was taken into another room, and I watched through a rectangular window. I saw a lot of urgent, even frantic activity, until what looked to me like a lifeless body was carried out. Then the nurse came out, crying, and she said, "She's going to make it." And she embraced me. I didn't know whether she was talking about my wife or the baby.

When the doctor came out, he stood against the wall, and then slid down, crouched, and said, "You can plan and plan, and then there are those 20 seconds of terror. But we made it." They had almost lost both of them. And the next thing I knew, they placed this little bundle in my hands. I looked at her face, and she opened her eyes. Everything changed in an instant.

It reminds me of that extraordinary passage in Marilynne Robinson's novel *Gilead*, which I read when we were making *Silence*. The dying minister is describing the wonder that he felt when he saw his daughter's face for the first time. "Now that I am about to leave this world," he says, "I realize that there is nothing more astonishing than a human face. It has something to do with incarnation. You feel your obligation to a child when you have seen it and held it. Any human face has a claim on you. Because you can't help but understand the singularity of it, the courage and the loneliness of it. But this is truest of the face of an infant. I consider that to be one kind of vision, as mystical as any." I can say, from personal experience, that this is absolutely true.

For you film is like a painting. The photography and the images have determined value. How can photography make us see spirit?

You create an atmosphere through the image. You place yourself in an environment where you can feel the otherness. And there are the images and ideas and emotions that one extrapolates from cinema. There are certain intangible things that words simply can't express. In the cinema, when you cut one image together with another, you get a completely different third image – a sensation, an impression, an idea – in the mind. So, I think that the environment you create is one thing, and that's a matter of photography. But it's in the joining of images where the film holds you and speaks to you. That's editing, and it's the action of filmmaking.

Commenting on Silence, *Ari Aster said that just by denying God Kichijiro became a true Christian. Do you agree with that?*

No, I think he might have simplified that. He is very articulate on the film in general, and Ari is a unique filmmaker who takes real chances. I think he may have been talking about the idea of what you want coming to you only when you let it go, when you give up control. This relates back to what I was saying earlier about the priesthood and my vocation. It's when you say to yourself, "I'm not going to hold on to it anymore, I'm letting go" –

and suddenly, that's when you receive the grace. I think that that is what happens with Rodrigues. With that action of stepping on the *fumi-e*, Rodrigues is basically embracing the mystery of life and death, which is what Jesus is. It's the great mystery, a great beauty, and we will never know the end of it.

In the process of living it, you come to the moment where you embrace it. And you try to do something that, if you're lucky enough to have the gift of talent and the obsessive drive to create, we can call art. It's a great gift. There's an essay by Flannery O'Connor where she quoted Thomas Aquinas, and she said that a work of art is a good in itself and what is good in itself glorifies God because it reflects God. That's true of any kind of creation. And art is, fundamentally, an attempt by us to make sense of our existence.

So, for me, it's not that Rodrigues embraces the mystery, but that he embraces the people around him and chooses to live with them. They don't have to die on the cross. They simply don't. Some people say that they are the real heroes of the film. I can understand that. Others come from the standpoint of criticizing me, and filmmakers in general, for being members of a cultural elite who take a little of this from Catholicism and a little of that from Buddhism or wherever else. And that I can't agree with, at all. When he steps on that *fumi-e*, he knows what he's doing. I remember the night when we showed the film to a group of Jesuits in Rome, and the first question I got was, "Would you do that? Would you step on it?" And I said, "Well, if Jesus told me to, if I heard Jesus tell me to step on it, I'd step on it." Was it really Jesus, or was it him talking to himself? Ultimately, that's not important. What's important is that he felt it from within, and that he was guided by the example of Jesus.

In the end, I think that *Silence* was a very special attempt at an understanding. Whether or not it's successful as a movie, I can't say. But it is a genuine attempt at an understanding.

Was this film inspired by other films, at least in some parts of it?

Really, I was on my own. I had to find my own way. But in general, I've been inspired by many films. Many Asian films. Many European films. Many American films. I live with them. They're with me. It's not really a matter of just this film or that film. Some of them I've gone back to many times – *The Searchers* (1956), for instance, or *Vertigo* (1958), or *8½* (1963). The Rossellini films – *Open City* (1945), *Paisan* (1946), and *Voyage to Italy* (1954). *Ordet* (1955), on the other hand, I've only seen once. I can't go back to it. It's so pure, so beautiful, so shocking. In every instance, you're spiritually transported and transformed. None of these pictures are a matter of mere entertainment.

Would you place any of your other films alongside Silence *to make a comparison either because it is similar, or because it is the opposite in its meaning?*

I suppose I could say that *Raging Bull* is similar. Jake LaMotta struggles everywhere all the time. No matter where he is – the ring, the gym, the street, the bedroom, the living room – he punishes himself everywhere and he also takes it out on everyone everywhere, all the time. Like Kichijiro. The difference is that Kichijiro is forced to do what he does, and Jake is not.

Mean Streets is similar, too. And maybe *The Departed* (2006) is the opposite of *Silence*. I was attracted to Bill Monahan's script because it was written from the perspective of Boston Irish Catholicism, quite different from what I grew up with. By the end of *The Departed*, it's a moral ground zero. There's no place to go but up. And the sacrifices of the characters, in particular the character of Billy, played by Leonardo DiCaprio. Roger Ebert said that it's as if you could hear Billy in confession saying: "I knew it was bad, Father, but I just couldn't help it. I was stuck. I knew it was wrong, but what could I do?" For me, it had a lot to do with September 11, examining our culture and our lives in that new light. It seemed to me that from that point, we had to start again morally. But we didn't.

Conversation Six

At the beginning of the pandemic, the predominant feeling in the lives of many people around the world seemed to be anxiety. Have you had to deal with that feeling too? How has your inner condition affected your creativity?

Back in February, when I realized that everything was coming to a stop – a "pause," as they said – and that my wife and I were going to have to quarantine and stay in the house for an indefinite period of time, anxiety set in. A new form of anxiety.

The anxiety of not knowing anything. At all.

Everything was up in the air, indefinitely delayed, and it was like a dream where you're running and running, and you never get where you're going. To a certain extent, it still is. When would it be over? When would we be able to go out? When could we see our daughter? And then, when could I shoot the movie I'd been planning so carefully? How soon? And under what conditions? Would the location be a problem? Would I be able to find a way to work with the actors and the crew? And then a specific question.

Which was?

If I couldn't make my movie, then who was I?

How did you live cloistered in your home?

The anxiety deepened, and with it the realization that I might not get out of this alive. I've had asthma throughout my life, and this is a virus that seems to attack the lungs more commonly than any other part of the body.

I came to realize that I could very well be taking my last breath in this room in my home, which had been a refuge, and which now became a kind of fortress, and was starting to feel like my prison.

I found myself alone, in my room, living from one breath to the next.

And then, something . . . arrived. Something settled over me, and within me. That's the only way I can describe it. And I suddenly saw everything from a different vantage point. I still didn't know what was going to happen, but neither did anyone else. I could very well become sick and never leave the room, but if that was what was going to happen then there was nothing I could do about it.

Everything was simplified, and I felt a sense of relief. And it focused me on the essentials of my life. On my friends, and on the people I love, the people I needed to take care of. On the blessings I've had – my children, and every moment with them, every hug and kiss and every goodbye – on my wife, and how lucky I feel to have found someone I was able to grow with and raise a child with. On being able to do the work I love.

I have felt these things before, but now I felt them with a greater urgency. Because here we were, suddenly living with the realization that the very air around us, the air that sustains us, could kill us. And for me and for my loved ones and my friends, the circumstances drew us closer together.

They cut through all the formalities, all the euphemisms for "friendship" and "community" that have sprung up around us on social media and that often seem more like filters or even barriers to the real thing. And then, something was revealed, bestowed upon us. The old habitual questions – "How are you doing?" "Are you okay?" – became immediate and crucial. They became lifelines. We found that we really were all in this together – not just in the pandemic, but in existence, in life. We truly became one.

Do you relate this discovery to something from your past, your work?

After I made *Raging Bull*, I found myself pondering a question. I'd gone through a whirlwind decade, I had poured everything of myself and my experience into that picture, I was exhausted, and I wondered: "Can I actually be alone in a room, with nothing but myself? Can I just be?" And then, so many years later, all at once, here I was, alone in my room, just living the moment, every precious moment of being alive. Of course I couldn't sustain it, but it was there.

What have you learned from this pandemic that you would like to communicate to a young person who is looking to the future during these times?

For young people, right now, I would love to tell them how fortunate they are to be alive at such a clarifying moment. Many of us think that everything will just go on the way it always has, and of course that's never really the case – everything is always changing, as this moment reminds us with such force. And it can inspire us to recognize our own ability to effect change for the better. That's what's happening right now with the mass protests all around the world – young people are fighting to make things better.

Have you been able to read books? What did those readings leave in your heart? And are there any authors who, in your opinion, help us to better understand what we experienced? And have you thought about a film?

During these months I've watched and read a lot, often based on conversations or suggestions from my friends – that's been precious to me. My wife and I took another look at *The Killers* (1946) by Robert Siodmak, and I was so moved by it this time – maybe it has something to do with Burt Lancaster's presence, the way he embodies such longing for the women he loves, and with the very special tone of the picture, which feels realistic and dreamlike, simultaneously. I incorporated a beautiful scene from *The Killers* into a little homemade reflection on lockdown that I made for Mary Beard's BBC show.

I went back to *The Brothers Karamazov*, and I read a selection from it for a literary festival that had gone online. I read Steinbeck's *East of Eden* for the first time at the suggestion of a close collaborator, and I was struck and obsessed by two sections in which one of the characters re-examines the story of Cain and Abel. He and his learned elders focus on the translation of the Hebrew word "*timshel*" and they discover that it translates correctly as "thou mayest" as opposed to "thou shalt." In other words, whether or not Cain will conquer sin after the murder of his brother is not a directive or a promise, but a choice – his choice.

With another friend I read some of Kipling's stories, and we were both stunned, particularly by "They." It's very far from the stories and poems he became famous for. He wrote the story after the death of his young daughter, and it's such a true and subtle expression of the tragic in life. Just thinking about it moves me.

And the other night, I looked at a film on the suggestion of another friend, *Seeing, Searching, Being* (2010), a portrait of the artist and spiritual teacher William Segal by Ken Burns.

There's a scene where Segal is speaking through his own stillness and meditation of honing your focus down to the essential, what's happening right now, from one breath to the next. Being. Breathing. Here. Now.

Isn't all of this Grace?

Conversation Seven

In the preface to my book Una trama divina (A Divine Plot), *Pope Francis made an appeal to artists to show us Jesus through "the genius of a new language, of powerful stories and images." You responded by writing a script for a possible movie about Jesus, which we've reproduced in the final pages of this book. You felt the force of a personal invitation; you had to respond, not with an essay but as a director.*

Tell me now, please, what struck you about Pope Francis's call to create?

Well, the church has played a crucial role for most of my life, starting in the 1940s and 1950s when I was growing up. And the challenge that His

Holiness raises in his preface to your book is something I started grappling with when I was thirteen or fourteen years old, and I've never stopped grappling.

The immediacy of Jesus... Whenever I tried to express the immediacy of Jesus, in conversations or in talks, and on a more serious level in my films, I found that many of the people around me were either not ready for it or they didn't accept it. What I mean is that I wanted the immediacy of Jesus here, now, not in the form of a beautiful and perfect figure, like the edifice of a church or a small basilica or a small chapel. Jesus doesn't only exist there. Jesus is with us, always. So how is that expressed?

This relates to a central question: can we be changed by others? Or does the change come from within us? This is what I've come to believe – that change always ultimately comes from within. You can try to force it from outside yourself, but it always comes from within. And for me, that change is always going to be guided by the words, the actions, and the presence of Jesus.

I tried for many years to understand how Jesus lives in the world around me, and how his presence could live in me and be expressed by me. For quite a long time I made the mistake of thinking that I was expressing Jesus when I was actually making a mess of things – it was a matter of pride and ego, of getting caught up in the role of the "big film director" and the power of making art. So, when you sent me Pope Francis's preface, I was excited. Because I felt that here was an opportunity to approach this question again, directly, as I had tried to do with *The Last Temptation of Christ*, to a certain extent with *Kundun* (1997), certainly with *Silence*. With *Silence*, I felt that I had found my way to grappling with the mystery in the right way.

So, in the introduction to this new script you wrote that you've been contemplating a movie about Jesus since the sixties.

Yes! Around that time, I came to realize that it's not about yourself and your own salvation, it's about being with others. Once I saw that clearly, I was able to see another passion that was in me, and that was the passion for cinema. Stories told through moving images.

I was taken to the movies a lot as a child. Looking back on it, I think I found myself drawn to images in part because in my family no one read books. My mother and my father both worked in the old garment district in New York, and I suppose they never had time to read a book. There were no books in the house until I started bringing them in. I had to learn how to read, how to live with a book. If the book was more than 200 pages, I had to learn patience.

I also learned by watching and experiencing everything through the life of the street and the storytellers on the street. They were wonderful – the ones on the streetcorner, the tough guys telling stories, always with a great sense of humor about themselves. My mother was a wonderful storyteller and so was my father, and so were my aunts and uncles. I learned and absorbed all of that and the only way I thought I could express this was through moving images, motion pictures. That's how I grew up: seeing moving images on a screen and looking at the art in the church: statues, paintings, crucifixes, stained glass renderings, stations of the cross – which were like a sequence in a movie. So, this question of exploring Jesus had to find its way to cinema for me.

That began in college. I went to Washington Square College, which later became NYU. But it was very far from the NYU of today, just a small campus in the center of Greenwich Village. It was a few blocks from where I grew up, but it was a world away.

I took film courses in school, but they didn't really show you how to make a film. You can't learn that in a classroom: it's more about the master and the student. We had a very good teacher named Haig Manoogian, who was Armenian American. He had a great passion for educating, he recognized that I had a great passion for learning. He saw something in me, and I followed his directions.

At that time, I wanted to make the story of Jesus: 16mm black and white, modern day, shot on the Lower East Side in the tenements and down on the Bowery, culminating in the crucifixion on the Hudson River Docks by the West Side Highway . . . which is no longer there.

Then, in 1964, Pier Paolo Pasolini's *Gospel According to Matthew*, as it was called here, was released. I saw it and I realized that he'd already done what I wanted to do. Pasolini's film was great poetry – new, modern poetry. The style was the style of the late fifties and early sixties, the French new wave, the Italian and British new waves, and primarily *cinéma-vérité*. The setting was period, but the style was new and immediate: he made you feel as if you were there. There was such raw beauty and power to those images. Pasolini gave the presence of Jesus a great immediacy, and his Jesus was not a movie star. God bless the movie stars, but they have a hard time playing that role. It was very hard for Jeffrey Hunter and Max von Sydow, in these lavish Hollywood superproductions, where every role was played by a guest star. I admired *King of Kings* (1961) and certain aspects of *The Greatest Story Ever Told*

(1965), but they were pageants, storybook versions of the life of Jesus. Pasolini's film was like a different planet. The face of Jesus was a face we'd never seen before, just like every other face in the movie. We'd never seen the setting before, the town of Matera; with the extraordinary mix of music – Odetta, Bach, Leadbelly, Prokofiev, the "Missa Luba" – that was completely new. And so was the strength of Jesus, the anger of Jesus. This was a great work of art, and I thought: if I ever get to make a film on Jesus, I'll have to find another way of approaching the story. So, for years I looked for a way of making a film about Jesus.

Out of that desire came The Last Temptation of Christ. *What's the meaning of that movie? It seems to be very carnal, visceral. I detect an obsession in it and something unresolved—*

Well, that film struck a raw nerve with some groups and sparked anger, resentment, ridicule.
 Let's start with the fact that it's a fictional version of the life of Jesus, not based on the

gospels but on a novel. And Jesus is a character. So, we're dealing with what this character does, what he thinks, what happens to him. He has to struggle to be the Messiah, he has to want to be the Messiah. And then, suddenly, at the very end of the novel, there's this beautiful idea by Nikos Kazantzakis, the author: Jesus is on the cross and he's tempted, not by power but by the ability to walk away and live a normal life, because this life that God has given us is so beautiful. The life around him, the tending of his garden, the love of a woman, a wife, children, raising the children – this life that the devil gives Jesus as a temptation is so beautiful that it's almost as if God envies the life he gave us humans. And I thought that was so beautiful, as an idea.

But the main point for me was to reconsider the way Jesus was presented to us in the mid-twentieth century in New York City, and probably throughout the country. We were taken to church as children. We looked up and saw Jesus on the cross. And we were told that he died on the cross for our sins. Okay. But what does that mean? I'm not sure. He is God, so he can die on the cross because ultimately, he doesn't have to suffer, because he is fully God and fully man. That was confusing: sure, it's easy for Jesus, but what about us?

When we suffer, it's different. We get angry. We misunderstand, and then years later, we realize that we've been wrong all along. We're afraid. That's humanity, and it's in Jesus too, all of it. It's part of his humanity.

So, we tried show the fact that he was fully human. Embracing death is absolutely terrifying, and that's why I had Lazarus's hand almost pulling Jesus back into the tomb with him, and Willem Dafoe as Jesus recoiling. He gets frightened because he realizes what he has to go through. The whole idea that it's easy for Jesus because he's God . . . well, no. Jesus chooses the way and it's very difficult. It was extremely important to me that I get that across.

There was another aspect that was important to me. I've read many translations of the gospels, and

I've studied the history of that time and place, the publicans, the ones who were tax collectors and what that meant, the prostitutes, the Sanhedrin, and so on. So, you have the Pharisees and the scribes saying that this guy is hanging out and drinking wine with prostitutes and tax collectors. Today, we think of tax collectors as guys with pens in their pockets, CPAs. But these tax collectors were thugs, extortionists, gangsters. In other words, he was hanging out with the worst kinds of people, and he was condemned for it.

When I did *Taxi Driver* (1976), I put a lot of those elements into the picture. We were shooting on 8th Avenue, between 43rd and 52nd Street. Now, it's prime real estate, just like my old neighborhood. Back then, it was the end of civilization. That's what it felt like.

That's what Jesus was talking about – the people who lived on the ragged end of civilization. So, with *Last Temptation*, I wanted to make a film for the people who say, "I'm a drunk, I'm a drug addict, I'm a prostitute, I'm mean, I have no heart, I have nothing in my life and nothing to offer, I don't deserve to be loved, Jesus couldn't love me." That's the Jesus I wanted for them.

The public reaction to The Last Temptation *was intense. What was it like making art in such a polarized political environment?*

I didn't assume any polarized situation. There were groups of people in America – Jews, Christians, evangelical, etc. – just different groups. Pre–social media. It seemed like an arena where you could make a serious discussion of Christianity. I thought there would be objections, disagreements, a civilized and intelligent debate, that would include some complaints. I expected that. But there wasn't a discussion.

Were you ultimately satisfied with The Last Temptation?

With *The Last Temptation*, I touched on all the iconography of the church: the Sermon on the Mount, Gethsemane, the crown of thorns, all of it.

And above all, the crucifixion. We were under stress throughout the entire shoot, just constant pressure. With the crucifixion it became extremely intense. In my mind, the film was never quite finished. The outcry started before we had finished post-production, and we had to release the film before we were ready to sign off on it. And on another level, is it really a movie? Or is it more of an attempt to look at Jesus and the iconography of Jesus in a new light and from a fresh perspective?

So, I realized that I had to go further into the story of Jesus. But there was a part of me that was compelled to deal with the iconography – I *had* to create the crucifixion, I had to create the raising of Lazarus, I had to create the Sermon on the Mount. I had to make my version of it all. But I think that in the end, that isn't really the story of Jesus. I did feel the presence of Jesus with me, but in retrospect I find that my approach to the making of the picture was self-centered. It was so difficult in the desert, and we were all so driven, but in the end, I felt that I didn't get there.

Can you talk more about what you mean by the "immediacy of Christ" in your script?

Well, if you look at Pasolini's Christ, sometimes he's just there in the corner of the frame, the one you don't immediately pay attention to – the first is last, the last is first. That was fascinating to me. The other films about Jesus that had been made up to that time were very, very piously made, and whenever Jesus appears he's the center of attention in every way. He's marked off from the rest of humanity in his way of speaking, his way of moving, his physical perfection, and in the framing, the staging, the lighting. It carries on a long tradition of representing Jesus in painting in absolutely idealized form, often with a halo. But what Pasolini did was to make Jesus a human being, a person, somebody you could get to know and talk to. This, I think, is the key.

The immediacy of Jesus, for me, is ultimately in our own life. It's the people around us, the tests we have in our own lives, and the strength Jesus gives us to get past ourselves and deal with others.

Something else struck me in this new script, how you wrote, "Jesus contains multitudes"—

Well, that's Walt Whitman. And Bob Dylan.

—Walt Whitman, Bob Dylan. Exactly, exactly. So, what do you mean by that? In what sense does Jesus contain multitudes? What kind of multitudes?

I think it's pretty obvious. Jesus embraces all of humanity, and Jesus really is all of humanity. He's showing all of us the way, the way to be able to live, to deal with anger and vengeance and retribution, with love and forgiveness and redemption and everything else within us and between us. He shows us the way. It's not easy, as we all know. But he is the example for the multitudes, because he is all of us. That is what I see.

Conclusion

What better way to conclude this book than to share Scorsese's contemplation of faith in the format through which he best expresses himself? The following screenplay was an integral part of these conversations in the sense that the idea of its drafting was born within them. This draft is a standalone work, representing the director's decision and need to "show us Jesus." A fundamental criterion in its drafting is the immediacy of the figure of Christ. For Martin, Jesus would never be represented as the King of Kings. Indeed, Jesus' divinity erupts from his humanity.

Script about Jesus
Martin Scorsese

I was deeply moved by Pope Francis's introduction to A Divine Plot, *Father Antonio Spadaro's book, and his call to artists deeply resonated with me. I wanted to respond, and I decided to do so in this form.*

We begin in darkness.

A painted image of the face of Jesus suddenly illuminates the frame . . . and just as quickly fades back into darkness.

CUT to a series of images: a plain wooden cross hanging over a neatly made bed in a tenement apartment . . . stained glass scenes of the life of Jesus . . . a marble sculpture of Mary cradling the body of Jesus in her arms ... a small gold cross next to a mass-produced image of Jesus praying to the heavens ... a boy sitting at a table looking up at the cross alongside elaborate full-color drawings for an imaginary movie called *The Eternal City*.

More images of Jesus: more mass-produced familiar portraits, brief moving images from *Intolerance* (1916), the silent *King of Kings* (1927), *The Robe* (1953), and the sound version of *King of Kings*.

VOICE: *Like millions of other children around the world, I grew up with images of Jesus all around me, all based on a common idea of how he looked and carried himself: handsome, beautiful long hair and beard, otherworldly, pious ...*

A clip from Pasolini's *The Gospel According to St. Matthew*: the Sermon on the Mount.

VOICE: *As the idea of making films became a reality, I planned a film about Christ in the*

> *modern world, in modern dress, shot in black and white 16mm on the streets of New York with apostles in suits in old, layered, weathered hallways, with the crucifixion set on the west side docks and cops instead of centurions – my world. But then I saw Pasolini's Christ. The setting wasn't modern, but the feeling was. The <u>immediacy</u> of Christ was there. Pasolini showed us a Jesus who was often impassioned and angry. Who <u>fought</u> . . . His film made the one I was planning somewhat redundant, but it inspired me to go further.*

An editing table. An image on the musty screen of an old editing table, which is stopped. Hands appear, take the film in hand and make a cut.

VOICE: *How do you represent Jesus in the cinema? I've thought about this over the years and made my own attempts. And His Holiness's words have given me a new urgency and another framework.*

The hand at the editing table goes to a canvas "bin," with numbered strips of film hanging on hooks along the top. One strip is selected, placed on the splicer, the tape is applied and the hand presses down the metal to seal the marriage of the two images.

> VOICE: *In the cinema, it's never just a matter of a single image. It's images in motion, but more importantly, images joined together. You take <u>one image</u>, you put it side by side with <u>another image</u>, and <u>a third image</u> is sparked in the mind's eye. And <u>that</u> is cinema – it communicates by way of an impression, or an idea created in the mind and the heart that doesn't exist in reality. It's in this eternal sphere, between the images of the real, of our world, where the presence of Jesus can be felt.*

CUT to Grand Central Station, New York City.

Constant movement from every direction, people exit trains and board trains, people rush to the subway, people search for other people, and some people just . . . go . . . A Bruegel canvas in motion, threatening to spill over the sides of the frame and envelope us.

> VOICE: *Jesus contains multitudes. He is constant. He is present in every effort when we're compelled to act from love, whether we're successful at it or not. He's there in every <u>inkling</u> of love. Not love for a specific thing or person, but love as <u>a source of power</u>.*

The camera flies through the crowds and slows with this face, then that face, then another and another – individual lives being lived *right here* and *right now* . . .

One young woman walks into the subway, where everyone stakes out their individual places and takes out their phones and starts scrolling . . . she's no exception.

VOICE: *In Matthew 10, Jesus says he's come not to bring peace but a sword. Is it a call to violence? Of course not. I believe that it's a call to look <u>through</u> any doubts and search for God within ourselves, the true feeling within all of us to act from love.*

The subway doors open.

A man gets on. He is filthy, unwashed, wears tattered clothing.

He pulls a cup out of a big, reinforced plastic bag stuffed with newspapers and plastic cartons and comes right at us.

He makes a speech – he's lost his apartment in a fire; he needs three more dollars to get a clean bed for the night – and then he sings in a grating voice.

He lurches forward through the crowded car with his big bulky bag.

Everybody is on edge. Eyes are averted. Some passengers shoot quick glances. Most keep their eyes fixed away from him.

He gets aggressive, even insulting.

The woman stays fixed to her phone.

It's almost her turn. He's coming closer.

Her money is in her purse, but . . .

. . . are the dollar bills folded under the bigger bills or is it the other way around? Wouldn't it be awkward if he saw her going through 10s and 20s to give him a dollar.

If she's the only one who gives him money, what will the people around her think? Will they judge her?

Anxiety.

He approaches. Closer . . .

Suddenly . . .

She looks up from her phone and directly into his eyes . . .

. . . he looks into hers. We hold on them, we stay *within* their exchange.

VOICE: *You surprise yourself, you really see someone and recognize their humanity . . . there is Jesus' sword, severing every tie with all the habits and alibis and unspoken behaviors that keep us at polite distances from each other . . . and going <u>right to the heart of love</u>.*

We remain there, with those faces . . .

VOICE: *Revelation can come anywhere at any time – in a boardroom, in the Oklahoma hills, on the yard of a maximum-security prison, in an airport or a Starbucks, in a museum or in a cardboard refrigerator box that someone has turned into a makeshift shelter, in a concert hall, or a torture chamber.*

The moment ends, the man doesn't bother waiting for money and trudges on, the woman gathers her things.

VOICE: *Life never stops. But that moment can open the door to real change. Yet, to step <u>through</u> the doorway? That's another matter. It's scary. Maybe that's why Jesus used the image of the sword.*

The woman gets off . . . and is swallowed up in the swarm of humanity. Bruegel again.

VOICE: *Painters, composers, novelists, choreographers, filmmakers . . . we keep trying . . . It's not a matter of looking for answers or making statements. We're trying to create something like life as it's lived . . . to give form to . . .*

what? To this inexplicable mystery, always changing. We keep trying, and we hope that we'll end up with something that expresses that mystery. For some of us, trying to describe what happens around those moments of revelation is at the heart of our work.

A clip from the 1945 French film *Le Père Serge*.

VOICE: I've always felt that there is no such thing as old or new in art – it's an ongoing conversation. And the stories and films that have inspired me are also part of this mosaic portrait. Like Tolstoy's story of an aristocrat disappointed in love who becomes a holy man – he believes he's achieved spiritual truth by locking himself in a cave, he has a violent realization that he's done nothing of the kind, and then goes out into the world, searching . . .

A clip from Bresson's *Diary of a Country Priest*: the priest interacting with the lying girl.

CONVERSATIONS ON FAITH

VOICE: Georges Bernanos's and Robert Bresson's story of the ailing country priest who fights to the death for the souls of his parishioners no matter how much they taunt and scourge him . . .

A clip from *Europa '51* (1952): Irene waving to the people she's helped from the window of the hospital.

VOICE: Roberto Rossellini's story of the woman moved by the death of her son to give all of herself to everyone in need, which results in her commitment to a psychiatric hospital . . . where she just keeps on helping others.

A clip from *Silence*: Kichijiro, coming back after another betrayal.

A clip from *The Irishman*: Frank asking the priest to leave the door open a little.

VOICE: We all reflect on the attempts we've made in our own work . . . the people who hover at the doorway to redemption, filled with fear and trembling . . .

A clip from *Raging Bull*: Jake La Motta in a ray of light in the Dade County Stockade.

VOICE: . . . and the people who somehow find themselves at the doorway and walk through.

A clip from *Mean Streets*: Charlie in church.

VOICE: The people who presume that they can choose their own penance and get off the hook . . .

A clip from *Silence*: Ferreira confronted with the *fumi-e*.

A clip from *Bringing Out the Dead* (1999): Frank carefully intubating the man who's had a heart attack.

VOICE: . . . or their own spiritual role

A clip from *Casino*: Pesci and Stone coming together for the first time, in a fever.

VOICE: *. . . or the people who live in a state of delusion.*

The editing table – the image from *Casino* freezes.

VOICE: *We try to find endings for our stories that give form to life as we all live it. Stumbling along, I realize I might be creating pictures that lead to more questions, more mysteries.*

A cut is made – the hands search in the bin for another shot – the shot is found – a splice is made – the film is threaded back into the machine.

VOICE: *So, what about the ending of this provisional film?*

CUT to Saint Catherine's Monastery, at the foot of Mount Horeb and Mount Sinai.

We follow a man, a woman, and a girl through the gates of the monastery, led by a guide.

VOICE: *A trip to Egypt I took with my wife and my youngest daughter.*

We walk down ancient stone corridors and around tight corners.

VOICE: *We're at the foot of Mount Sinai, at Saint Catherine's, an ancient monastery, a museum within – relics, sacred objects on display, so precious that they're lighted for only a minute at a time.*

We find ourselves in a small room in darkness.

VOICE: *I turn a corner – the light suddenly comes up . . .*

My face – stunned – between my wife and daughter, also stunned.

VOICE: *It's Jesus as Pantocrator, Byzantine, sixth century.*

The painting we glimpsed in the beginning, the light falling on it.

VOICE: *It was painted with the hot wax encaustic technique, which enhances and deepens its power.*

My daughter's face, almost terrified.

VOICE: *Its power to do what?*

My wife's face, entranced.

VOICE: *For whatever the reason – the time in my life, the fact that I was with my loved ones, the fact that we came upon it without any warning – of all the representations of Jesus that I've seen, this is the one that met me head on . . .*

My face, looking.

VOICE: *. . . that <u>commanded</u> me to respond. It had the impact on me that His Holiness describes, deep within. A question formed and came into being. <u>The</u> question . . .*

My face, my voice asking: "What does Christ want from us?"

CUT to the painting.

VOICE: *The question lingers. And this painting from the sixth century that looked deep into my soul, this very personal experience, opened the door to new images of Jesus, new ways of seeing Him . . . here . . . now . . . I believe that if I had such an experience, others can and will also find their own way to reflecting Jesus back to us in a new light.*

Light radiates from the painting, flooding the room and then the entire frame.

THE END